MathFlare

Name: ____________________

Class: __________

Teacher: ____________________

Introduction

As parents and educators, we recognize the pivotal role mathematics plays in shaping a child's academic journey and future success. Yet, the path to mathematical proficiency can often seem daunting, fraught with challenges and complexities. That's where the transformative power of MathFlare Workbooks shine through, illuminating the way forward with clarity, precision, and purpose.

Introducing MathFlare Workbooks – a beacon of guidance, a testament to excellence, and a catalyst for achievement. Crafted with meticulous care and expertise, MathFlare Workbooks stand as paragons of educational excellence, designed to nurture young minds, ignite a passion for learning, and develop a deep-rooted understanding of mathematical concepts.

Picture this: your child eagerly delves into the pages of Mathflare Workbook, greeted by a step-by-step guide illuminated with vivid examples that demystify complex mathematical concepts. With each turn of the page, they embark on a journey of discovery, encountering thoughtfully curated practice questions that reinforce learning and hone problem-solving skills. And when they unveil the answers to those very questions, a sense of accomplishment blossoms within them – a tangible reward for their hard work and dedication.

But MathFlare Workbooks are more than just tools for learning; they are pathways to comprehension, fostering a deep-seated understanding of mathematical concepts through a sequential, logical flow. From fundamental principles to advanced problem-solving strategies, every chapter builds upon the last, ensuring a robust foundation upon which future knowledge can be constructed.

As parents, we yearn for nothing more than to see our children thrive, to witness the spark of inspiration ignited within them as they conquer academic challenges with confidence and poise. MathFlare Workbooks serve as partners in this noble endeavor, offering not just practice questions, but the keys to unlocking a world of opportunity.

And for teachers, MathFlare Workbooks stand as invaluable allies in the quest to cultivate mathematical proficiency in the classroom. With answers readily available, instructors can focus on guiding and nurturing their students, confident in the knowledge that MathFlare Workbooks provide a solid framework upon which to build.

In the pages of MathFlare Workbooks, we find not just the promise of academic excellence, but the seeds of a brighter tomorrow. So let us embrace the power of mathematics, let us champion the journey of learning, and let us pave the way for a generation of young minds poised to shape the world. With MathFlare Workbooks as our guide, the possibilities are infinite, and the future, bright.

Table of Contents

MathFlare
Grade 2
MATH WORKBOOK
Step by Step Guide and Essential Practice with Answers
Addition Subtraction
Multiplication
Place Value and Expanded Notations
Geometry
MathFlare Publishing

MathFlare
Grade 2-3
MATH WORKBOOK
Step by Step Guide and Essential Practice with Answers
Addition Subtraction
Multiplication and Division
Place Value and Expanded Notations
Geometry
MathFlare Publishing

MathFlare
Grade 3
MATH WORKBOOK
Step by Step Guide and Essential Practice with Answers
Multiplication and Division
Decimals
Place Value and Expanded Notations
Fractions and Geometry
MathFlare Publishing

MathFlare
Grade 1
MATH WORKBOOK
Step by Step Guide and Essential Practice with Answers
Counting and Numbers
Addition and Subtraction
Place Value and Expanded Notations
Understanding Time
MathFlare Publishing

MathFlare
Grade 1-2
MATH WORKBOOK
Step by Step Guide and Essential Practice with Answers
Counting and Numbers
Addition and Subtraction
Place Value and Expanded Notations
Understanding Time
MathFlare Publishing

MathFlare
Grade 3-4
MATH WORKBOOK
Step by Step Guide and Essential Practice with Answers
Addition Subtraction
Multiplication Division
Place Value and Expanded Notations
Fractions and Geometry
MathFlare Publishing

MathFlare
Grade 4
MATH WORKBOOK
Step by Step Guide and Essential Practice with Answers
Addition Subtraction
Multiplication Division
Place Value and Expanded Notations
Fractions and Geometry
MathFlare Publishing

MathFlare
Grade 4-5
MATH WORKBOOK
Step by Step Guide and Essential Practice with Answers
Multiplication Division
Place Value and Expanded Notations
Fractions and Geometry
Unit Conversion
MathFlare Publishing

MathFlare
Grade 5
MATH WORKBOOK
Step by Step Guide and Essential Practice with Answers
Multiplication Division
Place Value and Expanded Notations
Fractions and Geometry
Unit Conversion
MathFlare Publishing

MathFlare
Grade 5-6
MATH WORKBOOK
Step by Step Guide and Essential Practice with Answers
Multiplication Division
Place Value and Expanded Notations
Fractions and Geometry
Units and Statistics
MathFlare Publishing

MathFlare
Grade 6
MATH WORKBOOK
Step by Step Guide and Essential Practice with Answers
Integers and Statistics
Arithmetic and Pre-Algebra
Fractions and Geometry
Ratio and Percentage
MathFlare Publishing

MathFlare
Grade 6-7
MATH WORKBOOK
Step by Step Guide and Essential Practice with Answers
Arithmetic and Pre-Algebra
Ratio, Percent Proportion
Geometry
Statistics
MathFlare Publishing

MathFlare
Grade 7
MATH WORKBOOK
Step by Step Guide and Essential Practice with Answers
Pre-Algebra
Ratio, Percent Proportion
Geometry
Statistics
MathFlare Publishing

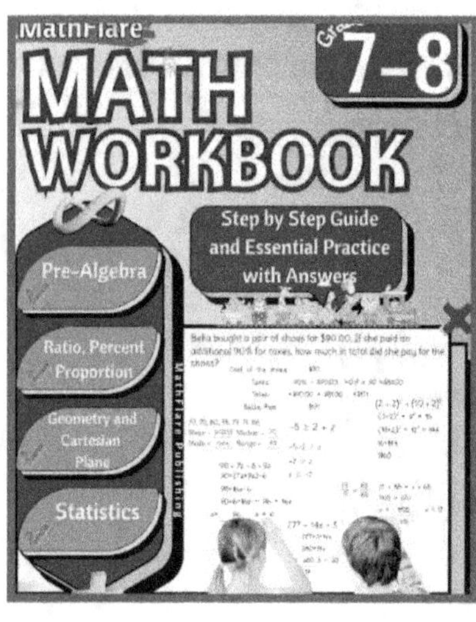
MathFlare
Grade 7-8
MATH WORKBOOK
Step by Step Guide and Essential Practice with Answers
Pre-Algebra
Ratio, Percent Proportion
Geometry and Cartesian Plane
Statistics
MathFlare Publishing

MathFlare
Grade 8-9
MATH WORKBOOK
Step by Step Guide and Essential Practice with Answers
Pre-Algebra
Ratio, Proportion and Percentage
Linear Equations
Geometry and Cartesian Plane
MathFlare Publishing

MathFlare
Grade 8
MATH WORKBOOK
Step by Step Guide and Essential Practice with Answers
Pre-Algebra
Percentage
Linear Equations
Geometry
MathFlare Publishing

Place Value and Expanded Notation

Place value tells us the value of a digit in a number based on where it's placed.

Imagine we have the number 643. It has three digits: 6, 4, and 3.

Now, each digit holds a special place:

- The digit 6 is in the hundreds place. It means it's representing six groups of 100.
- The digit 4 is in the tens place. It means it's representing four groups of 10.
- The digit 3 is in the ones place. It means it's representing three single units.

So, when we want to know the total value of the number 643, we add up the values of each digit based on its place value:

- The digit 6 in the hundreds place is worth 600.
- The digit 4 in the tens place is worth 40.
- The digit 3 in the ones place is worth 3.

When we add these values together, we find the value of the entire number:

$$600 + 40 + 3 = 643$$

Expanded notation helps us see the individual value of each digit in a number and how they contribute to the overall value of the number. It's like breaking down a big puzzle into smaller pieces to understand it better!

So, in expanded notation, we can write 643 as: 600 (from the hundreds place) + 40 (from the tens place) + 3 (from the ones place).

Let's solve problems from the exercises:

Place value of the underlined digit:

$$10\underline{1} = \underline{\quad 1 \text{ one} \quad}$$

Expanded Notations

26   2 tens + 6 ones

418   4 hundreds + 1 ten + 8 ones

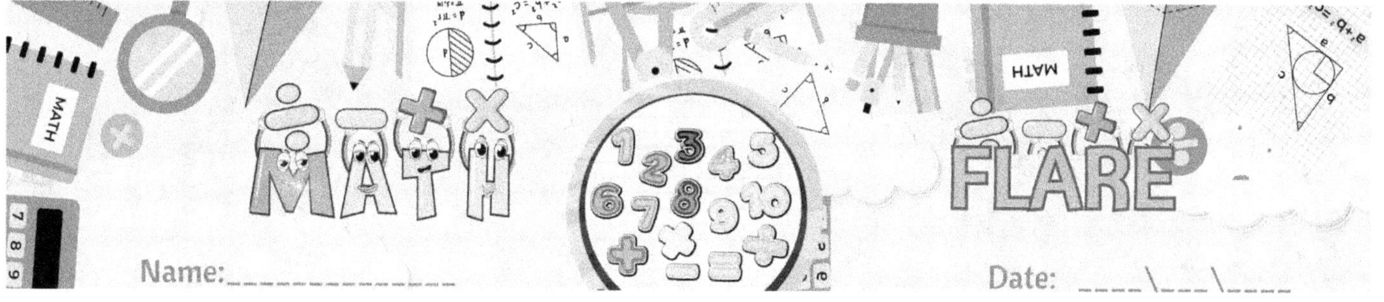

Name:________________   Date: _______________

Place Value

Determine the place value of the underlined digit.

1. 5,77<u>5</u> = __________________

2. 7,4<u>9</u>0 = __________________

3. 5,6<u>7</u>8 = __________________

4. 3,78<u>6</u> = __________________

5. 3,<u>5</u>41 = __________________

6. 4,<u>8</u>62 = __________________

7. 6,<u>7</u>64 = __________________

8. <u>9</u>,090 = __________________

9. 5,8<u>2</u>8 = __________________

10. 5,<u>1</u>14 = __________________

11. <u>1</u>,990 = __________________

12. 2,1<u>6</u>3 = __________________

13. <u>1</u>05 = __________________

14. 9,5<u>3</u>3 = __________________

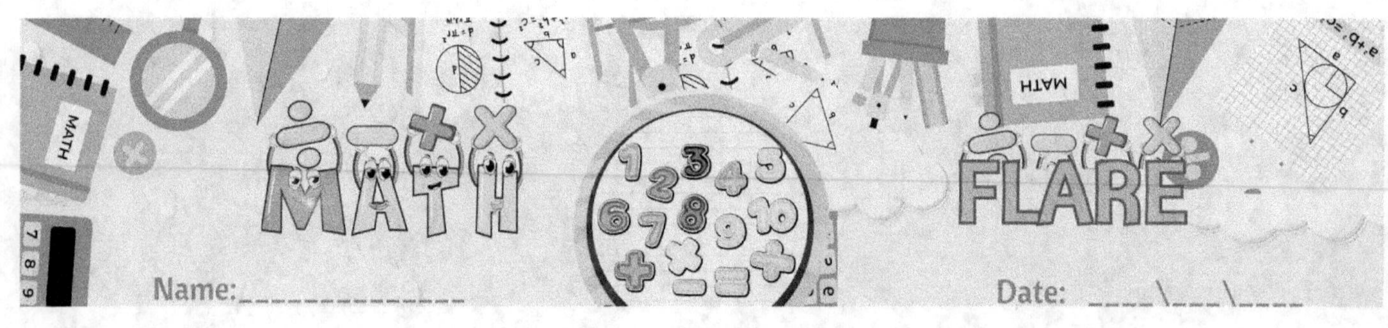

15. 1,4<u>1</u>1 = _________________

16. 2,<u>1</u>21 = _________________

17. 15<u>4</u> = _________________

18. 9,69<u>1</u> = _________________

19. <u>7</u>,288 = _________________

20. <u>4</u>,005 = _________________

21. 1,<u>0</u>83 = _________________

22. 8,<u>9</u>33 = _________________

23. <u>6</u>,834 = _________________

24. <u>5</u>13 = _________________

25. 2,4<u>5</u>1 = _________________

26. 3,72<u>5</u> = _________________

27. 9,<u>2</u>70 = _________________

28. 7,1<u>3</u>7 = _________________

29. 6,<u>3</u>31 = _________________

30. 8,<u>1</u>86 = _________________

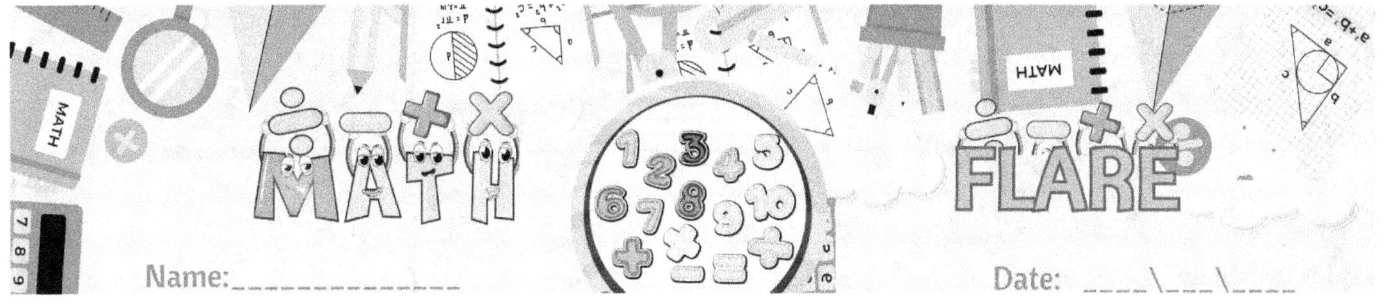

31. 3,898 = _______________ 32. 4,720 = _______________

33. 8,179 = _______________ 34. 4,460 = _______________

35. 3,302 = _______________ 36. 2,850 = _______________

37. 2,087 = _______________ 38. 7,340 = _______________

39. 3,565 = _______________ 40. 8,962 = _______________

41. 4,946 = _______________ 42. 799 = _______________

43. 7,604 = _______________ 44. 2,308 = _______________

45. 935 = _______________ 46. 5,397 = _______________

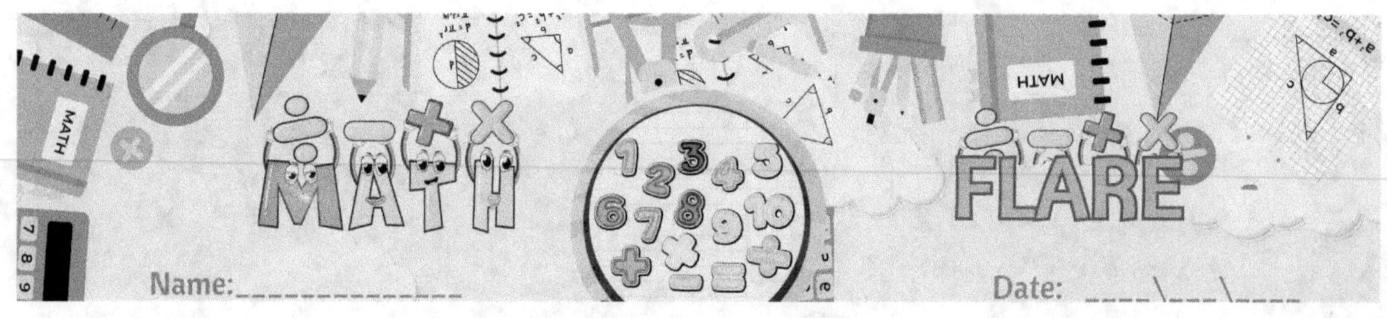

Name:______________________   Date: _______________

47. 5,858 = ___________________

48. 9,946 = ___________________

49. 2,833 = ___________________

50. 1,408 = ___________________

51. 3,256 = ___________________

52. 3,695 = ___________________

53. 6,865 = ___________________

54. 2,949 = ___________________

55. 3,314 = ___________________

56. 6,841 = ___________________

57. 658 = ___________________

58. 5,165 = ___________________

59. 1,336 = ___________________

60. 9,815 = ___________________

61. 5,591 = ___________________

62. 9,626 = ___________________

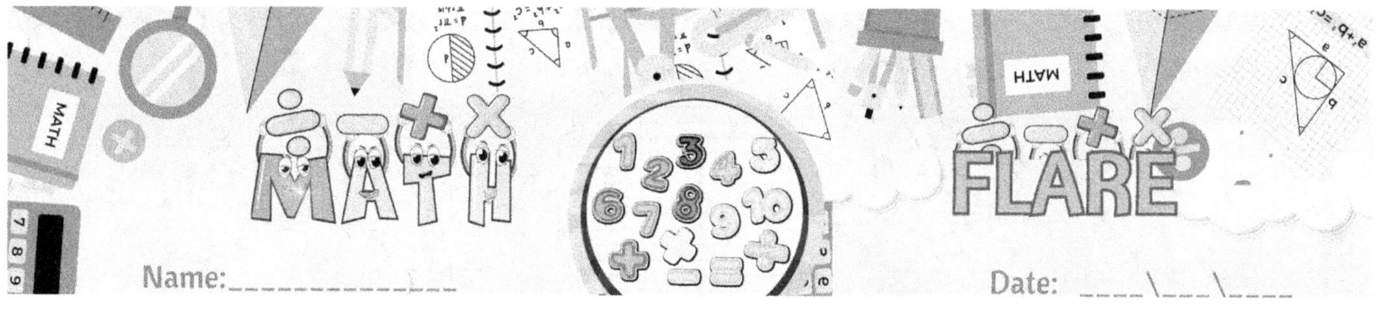

63. 2,7_60 = ________________

64. _7,641 = ________________

65. 1,_218 = ________________

66. 7,_269 = ________________

67. 3,9_83 = ________________

68. 5,64_5 = ________________

69. 6,_232 = ________________

70. _8,560 = ________________

71. _36 = ________________

72. 2,_814 = ________________

73. 6,12_7 = ________________

74. 8,32_6 = ________________

75. 9,_058 = ________________

76. _285 = ________________

77. 1,_330 = ________________

78. 4,5_26 = ________________

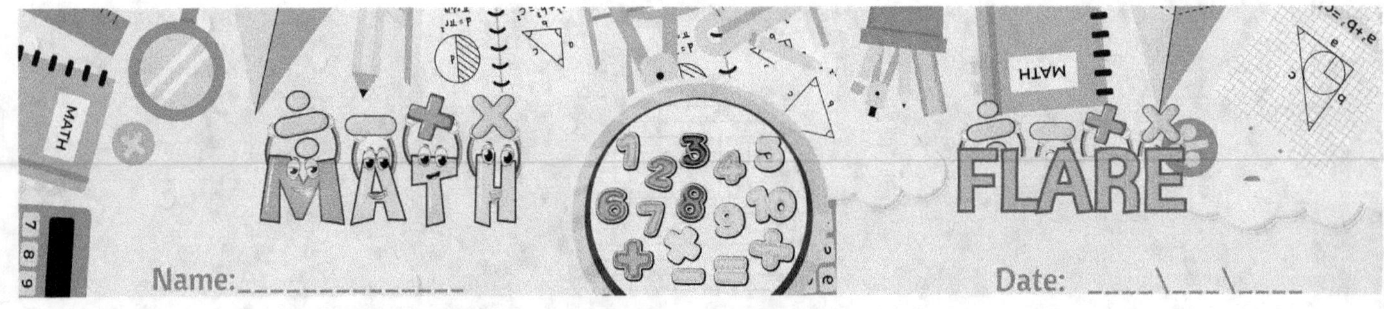

Place Value: Expanded Notation

Provide the expanded notation for each value.

79. _______________ 8 thousands + 5 hundreds + 8 tens + 9 ones

80. _______________ 6 thousands + 7 hundreds + 7 tens + 4 ones

81. _______________ 4 thousands + 2 tens + 8 ones

82. _______________ 3 thousands + 6 hundreds + 5 tens

83. _______________ 7 thousands + 4 hundreds + 1 ten + 1 one

84. _______________ 5 thousands + 1 hundred + 5 tens + 3 ones

85. _______________ 7 thousands + 4 hundreds + 5 tens + 3 ones

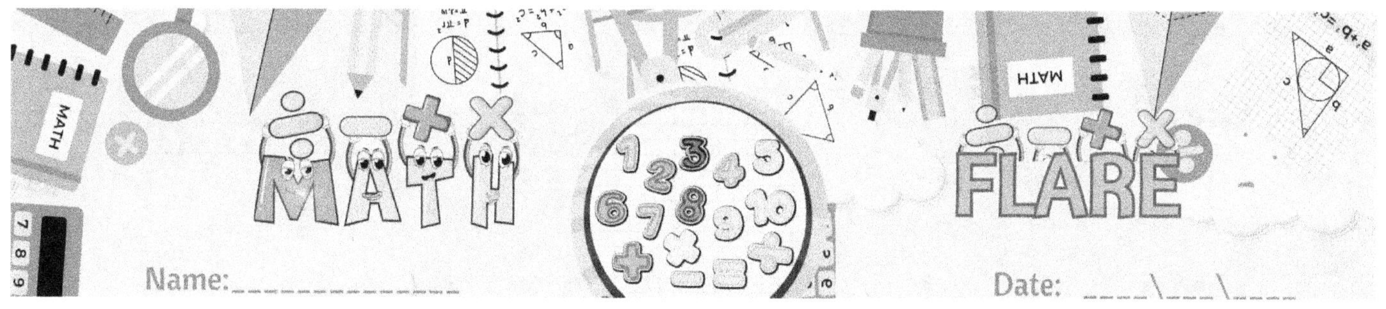

86. _______________ 1 thousand + 5 hundreds + 5 tens + 1 one

87. _______________ 6 thousands + 9 hundreds + 2 tens + 9 ones

88. _______________ 1 thousand + 6 hundreds + 5 tens + 9 ones

89. _______________ 7 hundreds + 7 tens + 1 one

90. _______________ 9 thousands + 7 hundreds + 8 tens + 2 ones

91. _______________ 9 thousands + 3 tens + 4 ones

92. _______________ 2 hundreds + 8 tens + 1 one

93. _______________ 3 thousands + 1 hundred + 4 ones

94. __________ 6 hundreds + 5 tens + 8 ones

95. __________ 6 thousands + 3 hundreds + 5 tens + 7 ones

96. __________ 6 thousands + 5 hundreds + 3 tens + 9 ones

97. __________ 1 thousand + 5 hundreds + 4 tens + 1 one

98. __________ 4 thousands + 3 hundreds + 2 tens + 8 ones

99. __________ 7 thousands + 3 hundreds + 7 tens + 6 ones

100. __________ 2 thousands + 6 hundreds + 2 tens + 1 one

101. __________ 4 thousands + 9 hundreds + 4 tens + 4 ones

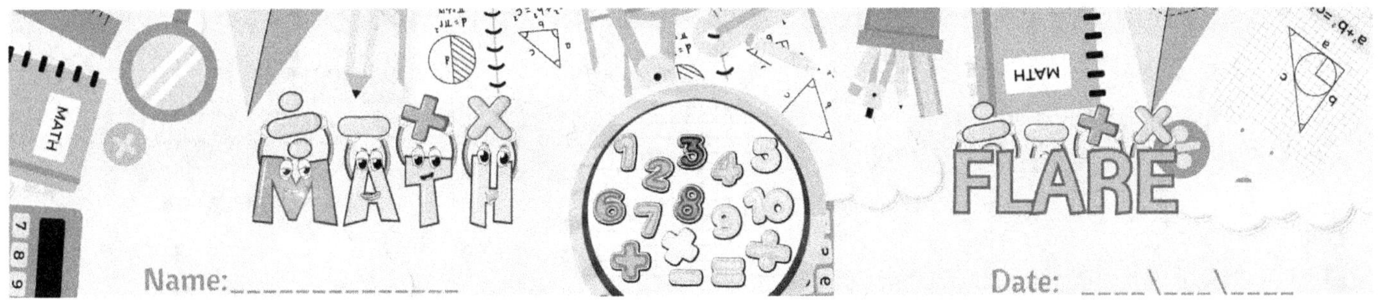

102. _______________ 7 thousands + 6 hundreds + 8 tens + 1 one

103. _______________ 4 hundreds + 9 tens + 8 ones

104. _______________ 7 thousands + 9 hundreds + 4 tens + 4 ones

105. _______________ 9 thousands + 7 hundreds + 4 tens + 3 ones

106. _______________ 2 thousands + 4 hundreds + 4 tens + 9 ones

107. _______________ 8 thousands + 6 hundreds + 2 tens + 7 ones

108. _______________ 1 hundred + 7 tens + 5 ones

109. _______________ 5 thousands + 6 tens + 3 ones

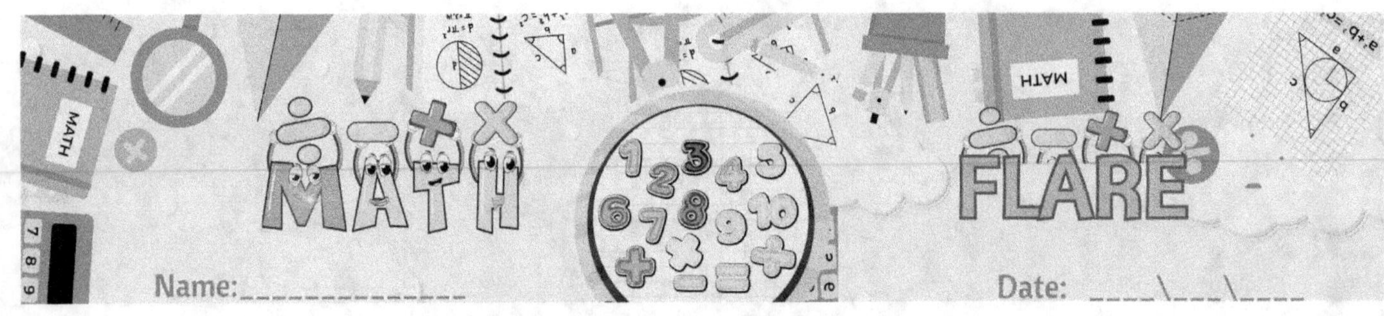

110. ______________ 8 thousands + 9 tens + 4 ones

111. ______________ 4 thousands + 3 hundreds + 7 tens

112. ______________ 1 thousand + 4 hundreds + 3 tens + 7 ones

113. ______________ 4 hundreds + 6 tens + 2 ones

114. ______________ 5 thousands + 2 hundreds + 4 tens + 3 ones

115. ______________ 2 thousands + 9 hundreds + 1 ten + 3 ones

116. ______________ 6 thousands + 4 hundreds + 7 tens

117. ______________ 4 thousands + 5 hundreds + 9 tens + 6 ones

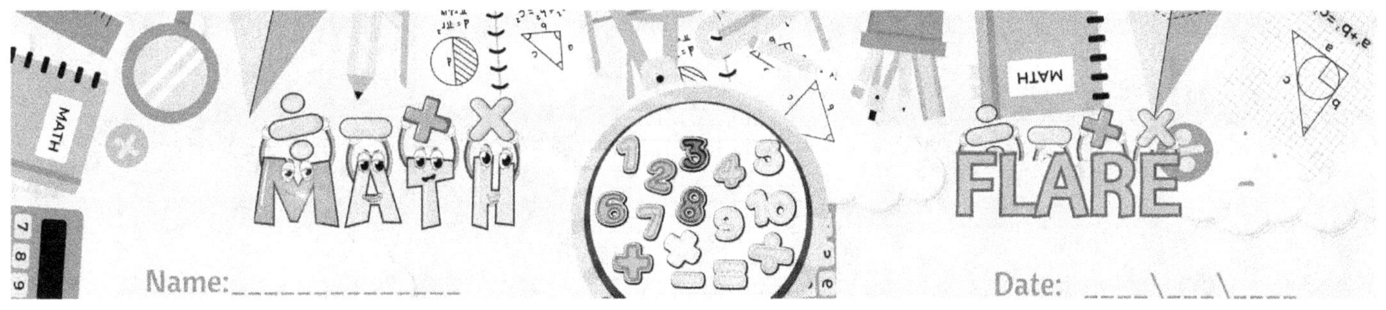

118. _______________ 7 thousands + 9 hundreds + 1 ten + 8 ones

119. _______________ 3 thousands + 9 hundreds + 5 tens + 2 ones

120. _______________ 7 thousands + 4 hundreds + 8 tens + 2 ones

121. _______________ 9 thousands + 1 hundred + 9 tens + 1 one

122. _______________ 3 thousands + 4 hundreds + 2 tens + 8 ones

123. _______________ 8 hundreds + 8 tens + 7 ones

124. _______________ 7 thousands + 7 hundreds + 3 tens

125. _______________ 8 thousands + 6 hundreds + 8 tens + 7 ones

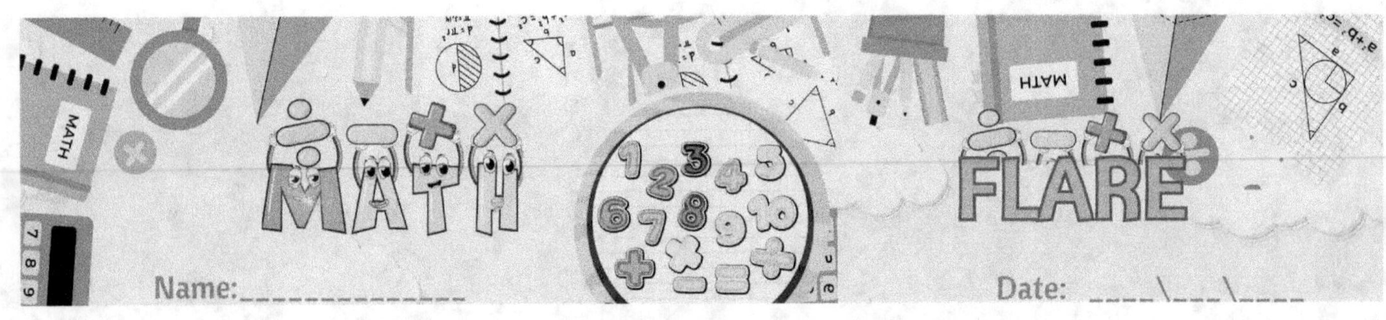

126. ______________ 2 thousands + 3 hundreds + 3 tens

127. ______________ 3 thousands + 4 hundreds + 4 tens

128. ______________ 3 thousands + 8 hundreds + 7 tens + 5 ones

129. ______________ 2 thousands + 4 hundreds + 5 tens + 9 ones

130. ______________ 5 thousands + 7 hundreds + 6 tens + 7 ones

131. ______________ 1 thousand + 2 hundreds + 9 tens + 6 ones

132. ______________ 5 thousands + 6 hundreds + 7 tens

133. ______________ 7 thousands + 4 hundreds + 5 ones

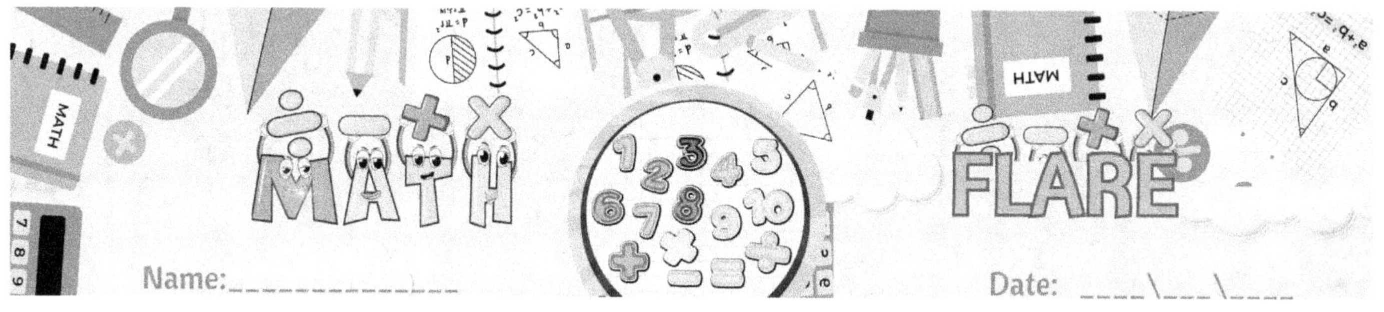

134. _______________ 5 thousands + 9 hundreds + 6 tens + 9 ones

135. _______________ 1 thousand + 8 hundreds + 3 tens + 1 one

136. _______________ 6 thousands + 3 hundreds + 4 tens + 6 ones

137. _______________ 3 thousands + 1 hundred + 5 tens + 3 ones

138. _______________ 9 thousands + 4 hundreds + 6 tens + 6 ones

139. _______________ 5 thousands + 4 hundreds + 9 ones

140. _______________ 5 thousands + 4 ones

141. _______________ 2 thousands + 9 hundreds + 2 tens + 3 ones

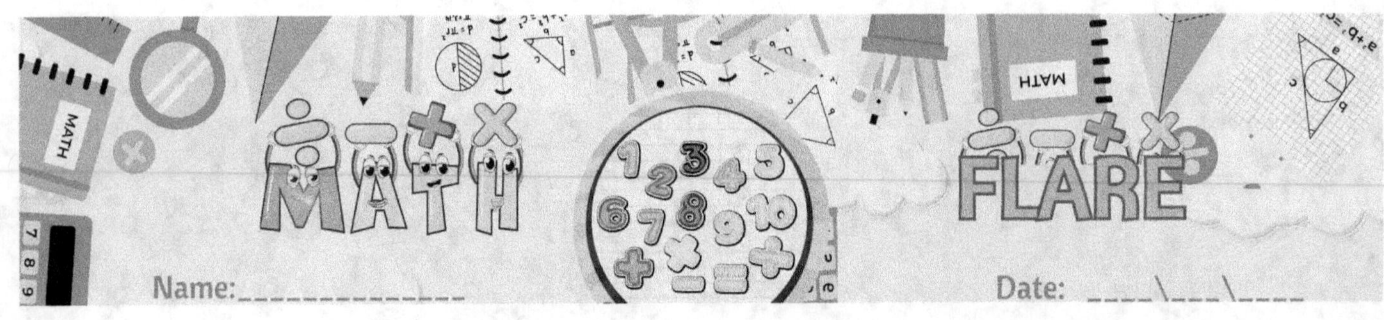

142. _______________ 6 thousands + 7 hundreds + 5 tens + 5 ones

143. _______________ 6 thousands + 5 hundreds + 9 tens + 5 ones

144. _______________ 2 thousands + 6 hundreds + 7 tens + 7 ones

145. _______________ 5 thousands + 4 hundreds + 1 ten + 3 ones

146. _______________ 7 thousands + 5 hundreds + 9 tens + 9 ones

147. _______________ 9 thousands + 8 hundreds + 1 ten + 8 ones

148. _______________ 7 thousands + 8 hundreds + 6 tens

149. _______________ 7 thousands + 7 hundreds + 4 tens + 4 ones

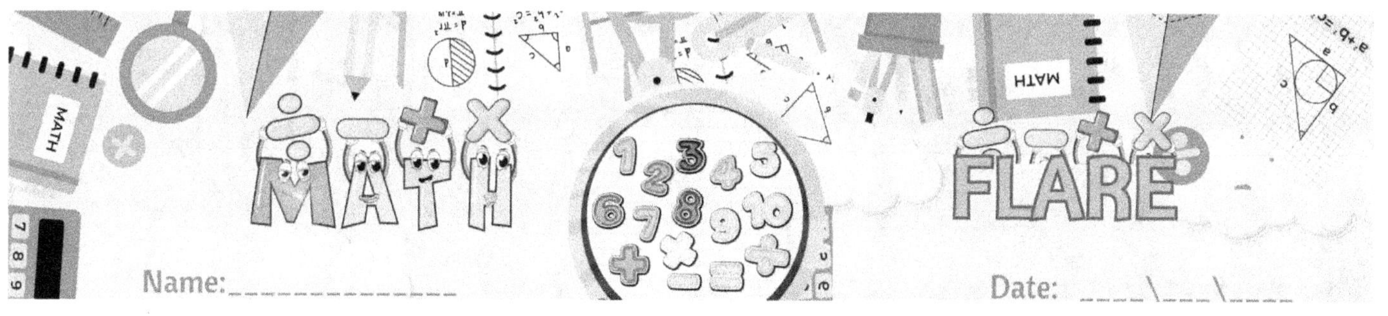

150. _______________ 9 thousands + 8 hundreds + 8 tens + 6 ones

151. _______________ 1 thousand + 9 hundreds + 4 tens + 4 ones

152. _______________ 3 thousands + 6 hundreds + 2 tens + 2 ones

153. _______________ 3 hundreds + 7 tens + 7 ones

154. _______________ 9 thousands + 8 hundreds + 9 tens + 4 ones

155. _______________ 3 thousands + 4 hundreds + 2 tens + 9 ones

156. _______________ 1 thousand + 5 hundreds + 1 ten + 6 ones

157. _______________ 6 thousands + 7 hundreds + 9 tens + 5 ones

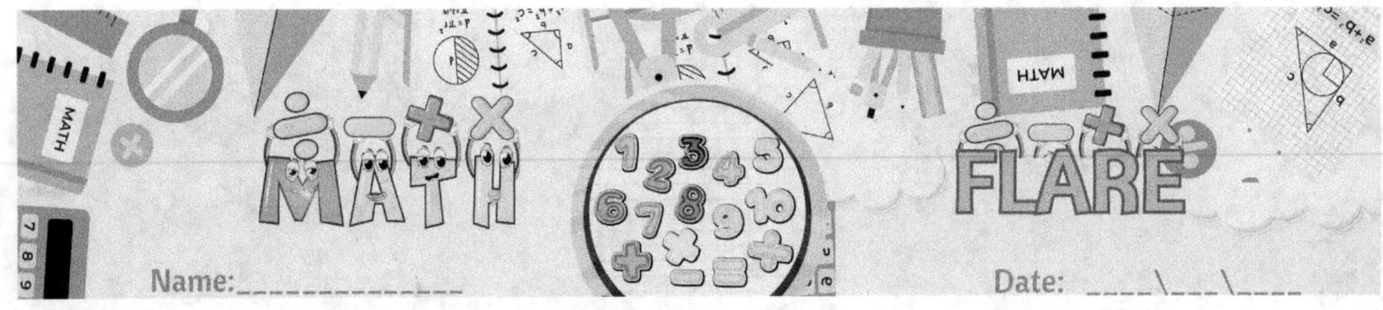

Place Value: Expanded Notation

Provide the expanded notation for each value.

158. 8,090 ______________________

159. 2,104 ______________________

160. 7,438 ______________________

161. 674 ______________________

162. 2,548 ______________________

163. 178 ______________________

164. 3,911 ______________________

165. 2,519 ______________________

166. 2,881 _________________________

167. 6,776 _________________________

168. 3,353 _________________________

169. 2,604 _________________________

170. 4,153 _________________________

171. 1,117 _________________________

172. 6,445 _________________________

173. 6,980 _________________________

174. 1,342 _________________________

175. 7,901 _________________________

176. 1,486 _______________________

177. 6,048 _______________________

178. 120 _______________________

179. 967 _______________________

180. 4,750 _______________________

181. 4,349 _______________________

182. 1,395 _______________________

183. 8,530 _______________________

184. 7,769 _______________________

185. 834 _______________________

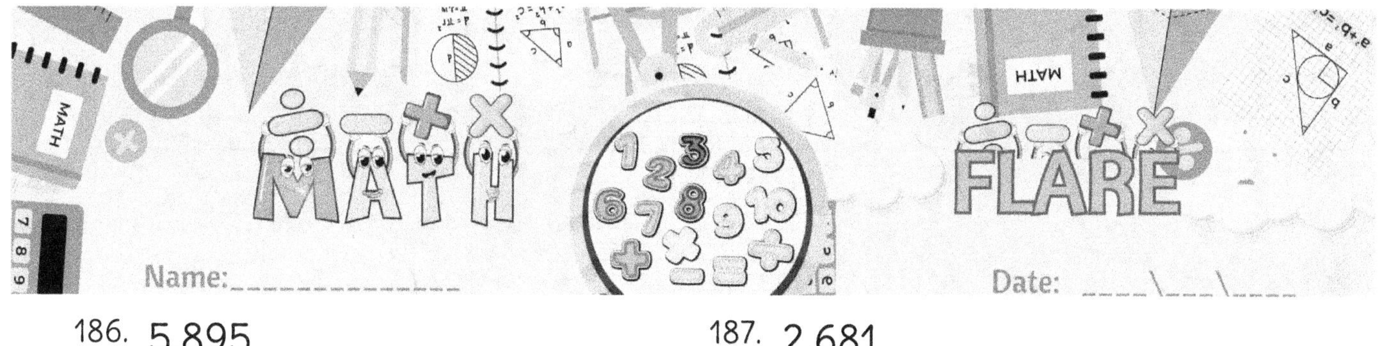

186. 5,895 _______________

187. 2,681 _______________

188. 1,722 _______________

189. 6,093 _______________

190. 4,786 _______________

191. 7,296 _______________

192. 1,126 _______________

193. 5,866 _______________

194. 3,046 _______________

195. 4,038 _______________

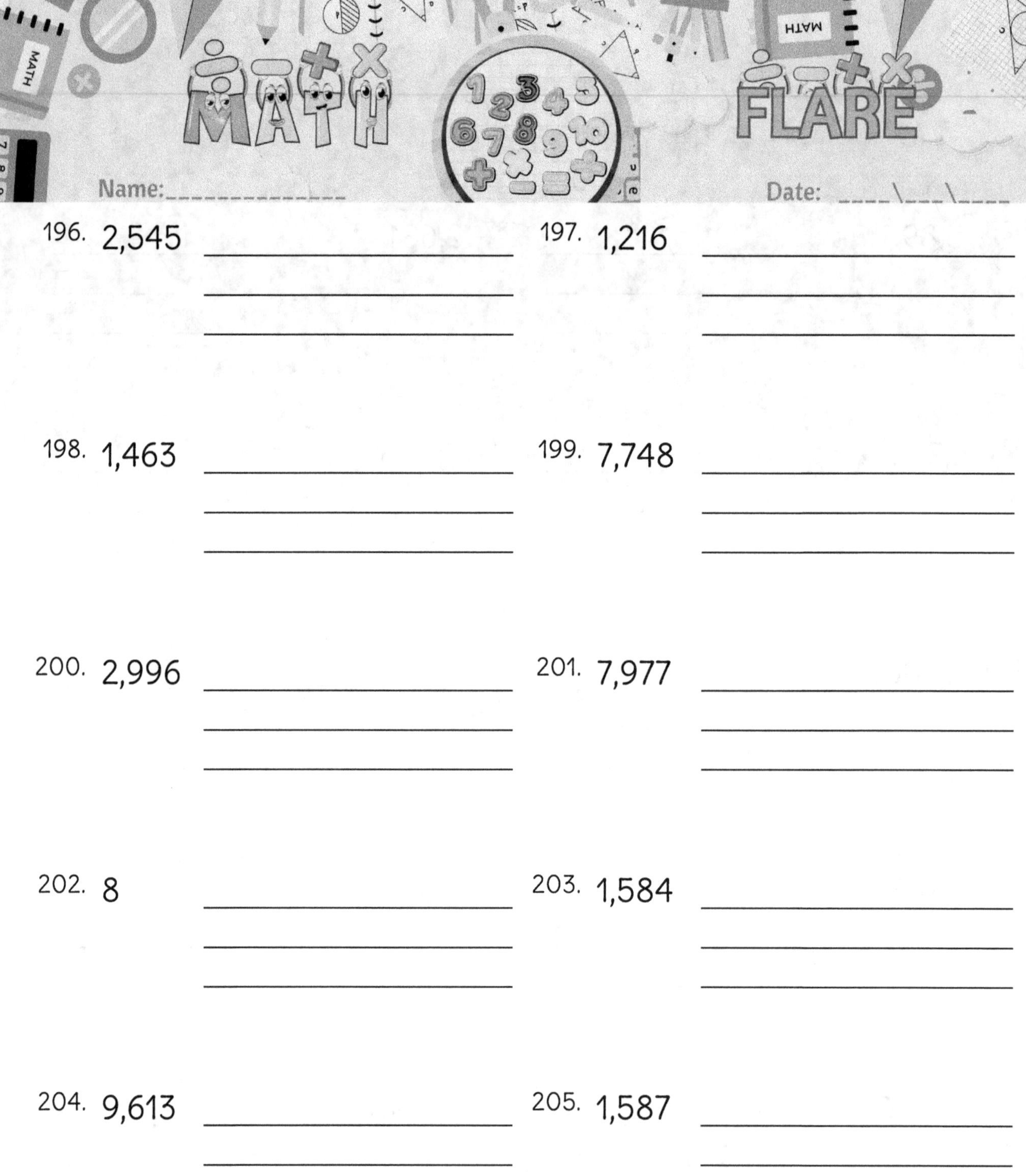

196. 2,545 _______________

197. 1,216 _______________

198. 1,463 _______________

199. 7,748 _______________

200. 2,996 _______________

201. 7,977 _______________

202. 8 _______________

203. 1,584 _______________

204. 9,613 _______________

205. 1,587 _______________

206. 6,528 ___________________
____
____

207. 6,904 ___________________
____
____

208. 6,769 ___________________
____
____

209. 2,743 ___________________
____
____

210. 7,533 ___________________
____
____

211. 9,127 ___________________
____
____

212. 7,971 ___________________
____
____

213. 1,138 ___________________
____
____

214. 3,341 ___________________
____
____

215. 3,090 ___________________
____
____

216. 9,278 __________________

217. 4,018 __________________

218. 2,408 __________________

219. 3,078 __________________

220. 6,623 __________________

221. 202 __________________

222. 5,055 __________________

223. 7,259 __________________

224. 7,816 __________________

225. 6,856 __________________

226. 9,990 _______________________

227. 580 _______________________

228. 3,935 _______________________

229. 7,302 _______________________

230. 5,357 _______________________

231. 271 _______________________

232. 4,587 _______________________

233. 2,372 _______________________

234. 7,970 _______________________

235. 6,772 _______________________

Place Value: Expanded Notation

Provide the expanded notation for each value.

236. __________ 4,000 + 300 + 40 + 2

237. __________ 9,000 + 800 + 10

238. __________ 8,000 + 900 + 10 + 6

239. __________ 6,000 + 100 + 80 + 3

240. __________ 4,000 + 300 + 5

241. __________ 8,000 + 900 + 90

242. __________ 5,000 + 900 + 10 + 1

243. __________ 8,000 + 900 + 70 + 8

244. __________ 8,000 + 500 + 50 + 9

245. __________ 5,000 + 600 + 50 + 8

246. __________ 9,000 + 300 + 20 + 4

247. __________ 9,000 + 900 + 80 + 7

248. __________ 2,000 + 500 + 20 + 6

249. __________ 9,000 + 900 + 50 + 5

250. __________ 4,000 + 700 + 50 + 9

251. __________ 8,000 + 500 + 20 + 6

252. __________ 8,000 + 800 + 7

253. __________ 8,000 + 300 + 80 + 4

254. __________ 1,000 + 100 + 20 + 5

255. __________ 2,000 + 700 + 90 + 5

256. __________ 2,000 + 900 + 20 + 3

257. __________ 2,000 + 700 + 40 + 8

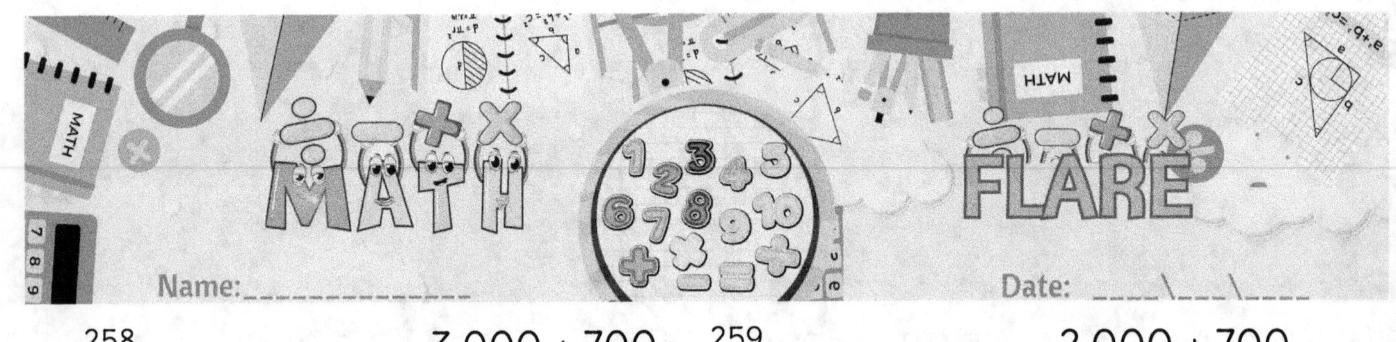

258. ____________ 3,000 + 700 + 60 + 7

259. ____________ 2,000 + 700 + 50 + 8

260. ____________ 1,000 + 500 + 90 + 6

261. ____________ 5,000 + 900 + 40 + 9

262. ____________ 2,000 + 900 + 70

263. ____________ 9,000 + 400 + 60 + 6

264. ____________ 7,000 + 300 + 80 + 5

265. ____________ 7,000 + 200 + 60 + 3

266. ____________ 4,000 + 500 + 40 + 1

267. ____________ 5,000 + 600

268. ____________ 3,000 + 100 + 60 + 8

269. ____________ 6,000 + 500 + 60 + 8

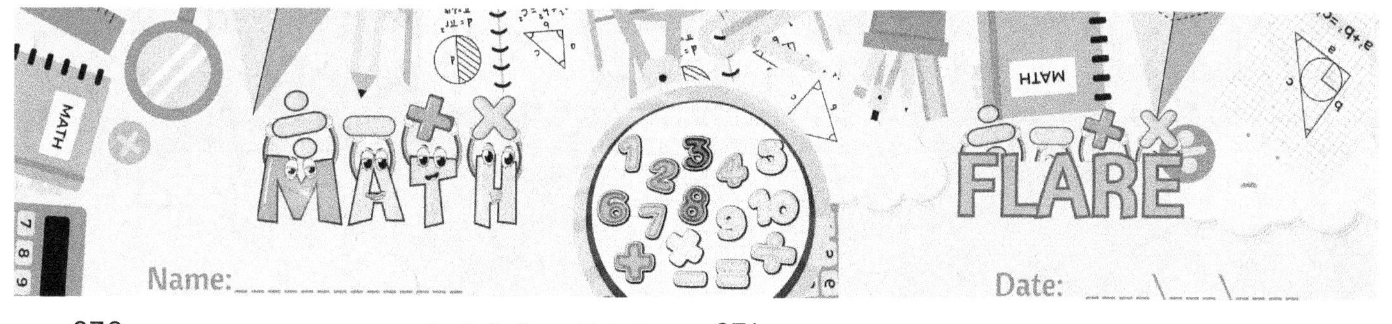

270. _____________ 8,000 + 700 + 40 + 6

271. _____________ 9,000 + 400 + 60 + 7

272. _____________ 5,000 + 100 + 1

273. _____________ 6,000 + 200 + 20 + 4

274. _____________ 8,000 + 700 + 70 + 2

275. _____________ 7,000 + 600 + 30 + 3

276. _____________ 4,000 + 200 + 90

277. _____________ 6,000 + 70 + 6

278. _____________ 8,000 + 700

279. _____________ 2,000 + 100 + 50 + 9

280. _____________ 7,000 + 500 + 30 + 1

281. _____________ 4

282. ___________ 8,000 + 50 + 3

283. ___________ 3,000 + 900 + 70 + 9

284. ___________ 2,000 + 500 + 40 + 4

285. ___________ 6,000 + 800 + 30

286. ___________ 1,000 + 400 + 60 + 3

287. ___________ 6,000 + 200 + 1

288. ___________ 1,000 + 200 + 40 + 7

289. ___________ 5,000 + 100 + 70 + 5

290. ___________ 3,000 + 800 + 50 + 1

291. ___________ 1,000 + 500 + 90 + 5

292. ___________ 6,000 + 40 + 5

293. ___________ 6,000 + 100 + 50 + 9

294. _______________ 4,000 + 500 + 80 + 8

295. _______________ 8,000 + 300 + 50 + 5

Place Value: Expanded Notation

Provide the expanded notation for each value.

296. 1,322 _______________

297. 5,713 _______________

298. 9,604 _______________

299. 8,985 _______________

300. 8,008 _______________

301. 8,640 _______________

302. 9,956 _______________

303. 4,583 _______________

304. 8,323 _________________

305. 3,444 _________________

306. 1,910 _________________

307. 8,263 _________________

308. 4,436 _________________

309. 4,354 _________________

310. 8,855 _________________

311. 8,712 _________________

312. 5,383 _________________

313. 8,919 _________________

314. 7,932 _________________

315. 7,394 _________________

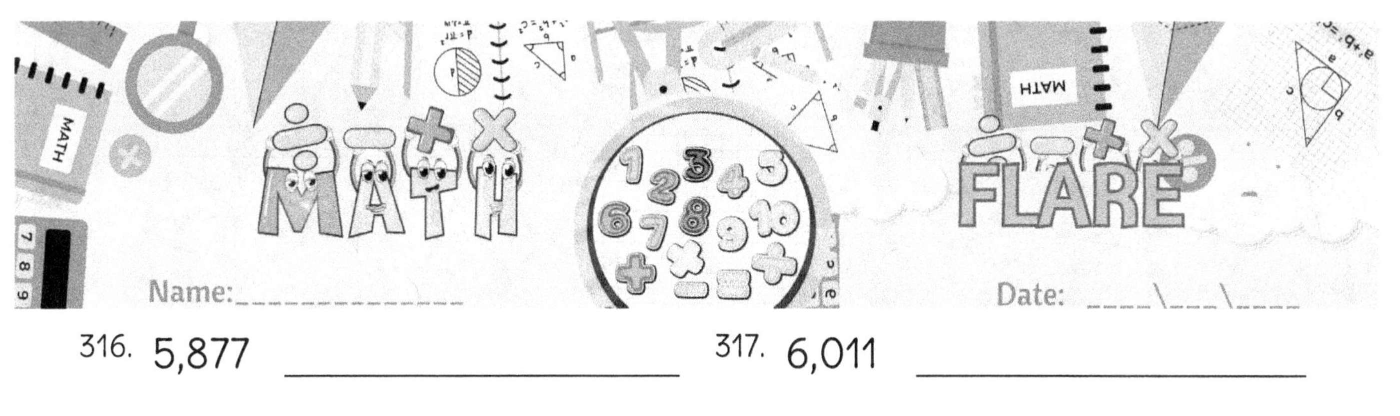

316. 5,877 ___________________
____

317. 6,011 ___________________
____

318. 4,639 ___________________
____

319. 906 ___________________
____

320. 3,870 ___________________
____

321. 9,513 ___________________
____

322. 4,585 ___________________
____

323. 4,660 ___________________
____

324. 809 ___________________
____

325. 9,850 ___________________
____

326. 3,888 ___________________
____

327. 8,572 ___________________
____

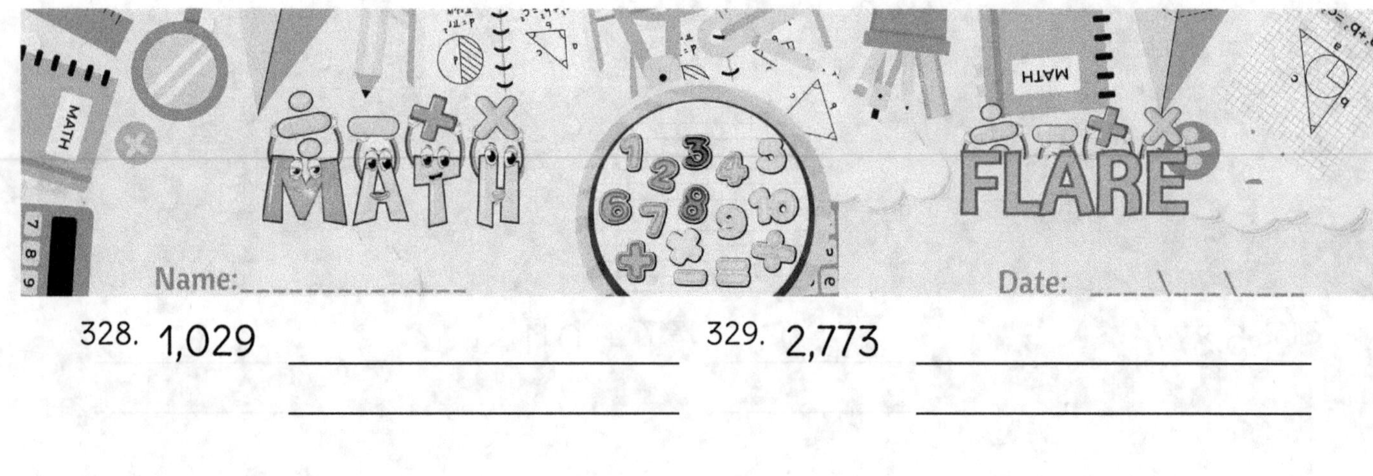

328. 1,029 ___________________

329. 2,773 ___________________

330. 7,507 ___________________

331. 7,526 ___________________

332. 4,452 ___________________

333. 2,884 ___________________

334. 6,475 ___________________

335. 2,306 ___________________

336. 9,237 ___________________

337. 7,296 ___________________

338. 2,336 ___________________

339. 8,920 ___________________

340. 4,733 _______________

341. 2,304 _______________

342. 6,983 _______________

343. 4,057 _______________

344. 6,944 _______________

345. 7,508 _______________

346. 4,289 _______________

347. 8,230 _______________

348. 8,989 _______________

349. 4,355 _______________

350. 722 _______________

351. 5,311 _______________

352. 1,075 ___________________________

353. 8,700 ___________________________

354. 5,115 ___________________________

355. 8,493 ___________________________

356. 4,056 ___________________________

357. 5,297 ___________________________

358. 3,774 ___________________________

359. 8,473 ___________________________

360. 9,555 ___________________________

361. 3,337 ___________________________

362. 7,235 ___________________________

363. 1,664 ___________________________

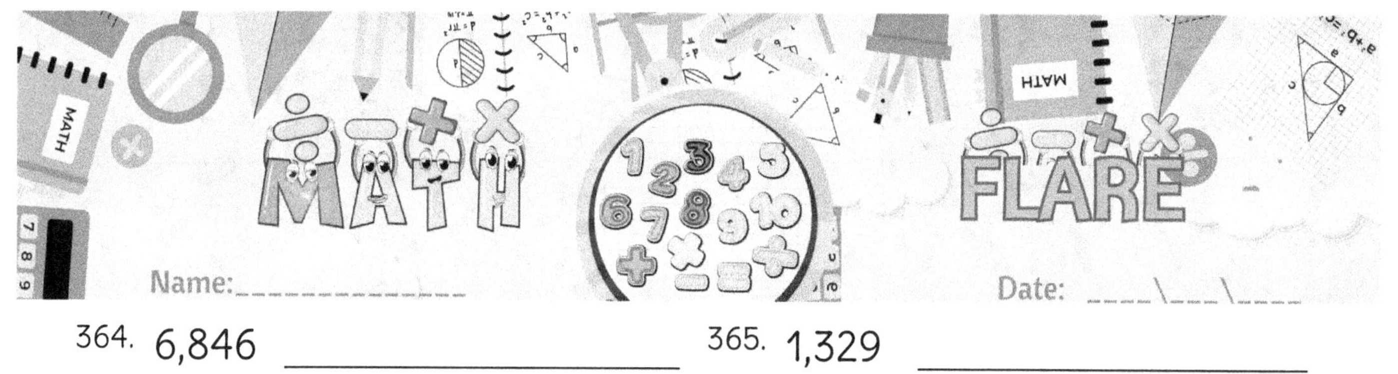

Name:________________   Date: ____________

364. 6,846 _______________________

365. 1,329 _______________________

366. 4,261 _______________________

367. 2,499 _______________________

368. 2,445 _______________________

369. 5,626 _______________________

370. 8,156 _______________________

371. 8,580 _______________________

372. 3,676 _______________________

373. 5,718 _______________________

374. 6,172 _______________________

375. 1,567 _______________________

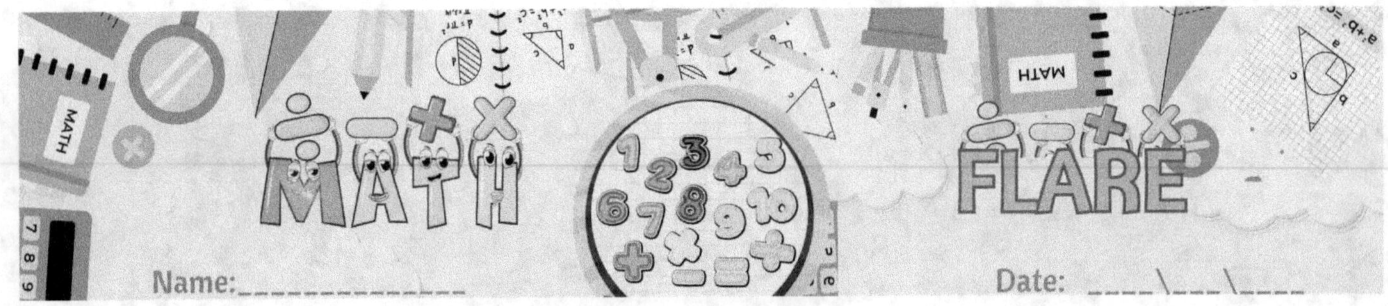

Place Value: Expanded Notation

Provide the expanded notation for each value.

376. _________________ five thousand six hundred thirty-three

377. _________________ one thousand three hundred eight

378. _________________ two thousand four hundred thirty

379. _________________ six thousand one hundred ninety-six

380. _________________ nine thousand seven hundred thirty-two

381. _________________ four thousand six hundred three

382. _________________ eight thousand three hundred sixty-five

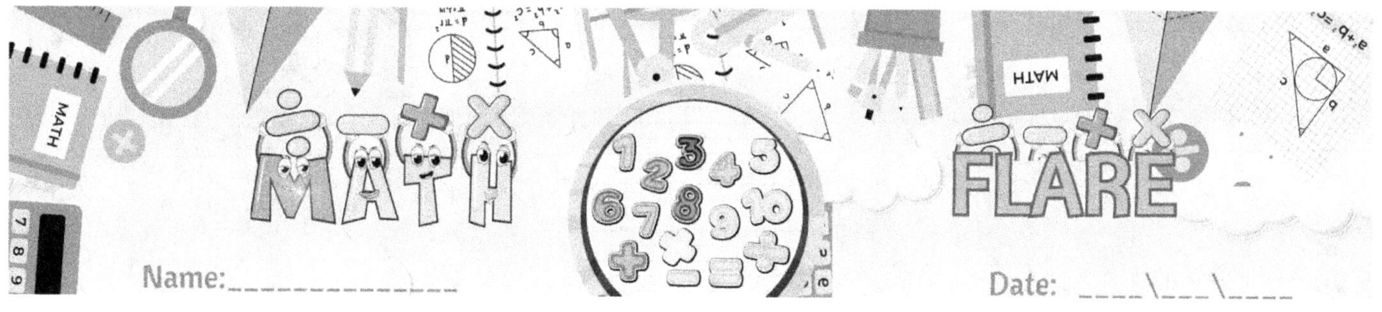

383. ____________ four thousand four hundred seventy-six

384. ____________ seven thousand forty-four

385. ____________ seven thousand two hundred ten

386. ____________ two thousand nine hundred fifty-two

387. ____________ eight thousand five hundred fifty-three

388. ____________ three thousand six hundred fifty-one

389. ____________ five thousand two hundred eighty

390. ____________ one thousand five hundred seventy

391. _______________ six thousand four hundred thirty-six

392. _______________ two thousand five hundred sixty-five

393. _______________ one thousand eight hundred thirty-seven

394. _______________ nine thousand seven hundred sixty-eight

395. _______________ three thousand eight hundred fifty-nine

396. _______________ nine thousand eight hundred sixty-two

397. _______________ seven thousand thirty-six

398. _______________ seven thousand eight hundred thirty-three

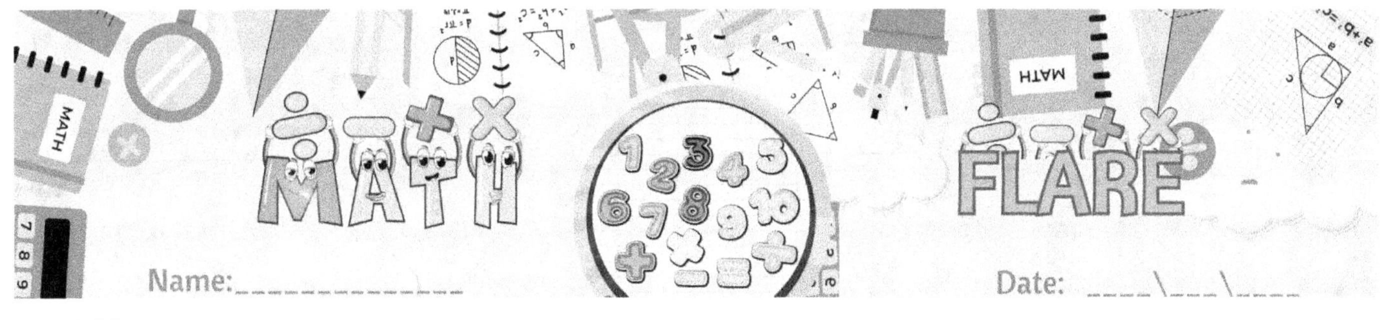

399. _____________ one thousand seventy-two

400. _____________ four thousand two hundred eighty-nine

401. _____________ three thousand seven hundred eighty-two

402. _____________ nine thousand six hundred twelve

403. _____________ three thousand three hundred ninety-six

404. _____________ one thousand seven hundred seventeen

405. _____________ three thousand nine hundred fifty-two

406. _____________ five thousand five hundred fifty-one

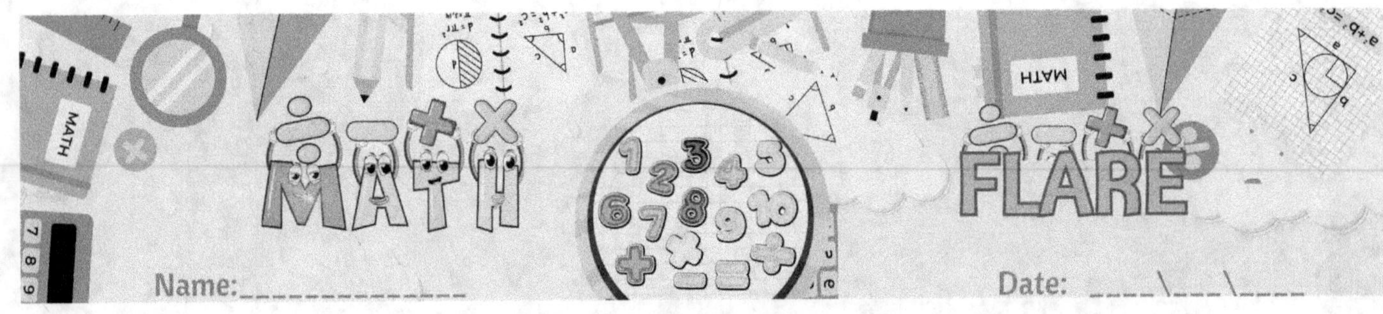

407. _____________ nine thousand eighty-five

408. _____________ five thousand six hundred sixteen

409. _____________ eight thousand four hundred thirty-five

410. _____________ nine thousand one hundred twenty-three

411. _____________ three thousand seven hundred fifty-seven

412. _____________ three thousand eight hundred sixteen

413. _____________ four thousand nine hundred forty-nine

414. _____________ four thousand seven hundred sixty-six

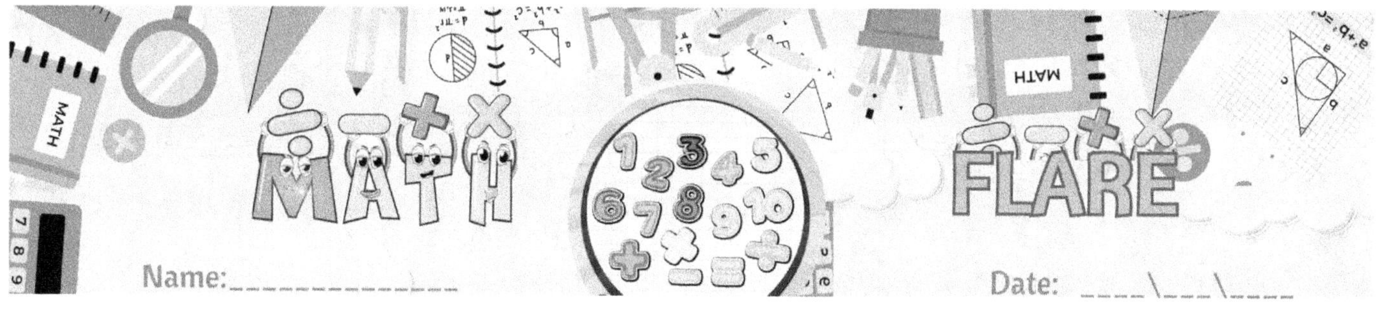

415. ___________ six thousand six hundred forty-two

416. ___________ six thousand three hundred thirty-three

417. ___________ four thousand forty

418. ___________ eight thousand four hundred thirty-two

419. ___________ one thousand seven hundred twenty-seven

420. ___________ seven thousand eighty-five

421. ___________ four thousand nine hundred twelve

422. ___________ four thousand four hundred seventy-four

423. ______________ nine thousand ninety-one

424. ______________ nine thousand seven hundred twenty-two

425. ______________ five thousand ninety-two

426. ______________ seven thousand one hundred thirty-two

427. ______________ eight hundred seventy-four

428. ______________ six thousand four hundred twenty

429. ______________ eight thousand six hundred twenty-one

430. ______________ eight thousand five hundred ninety-five

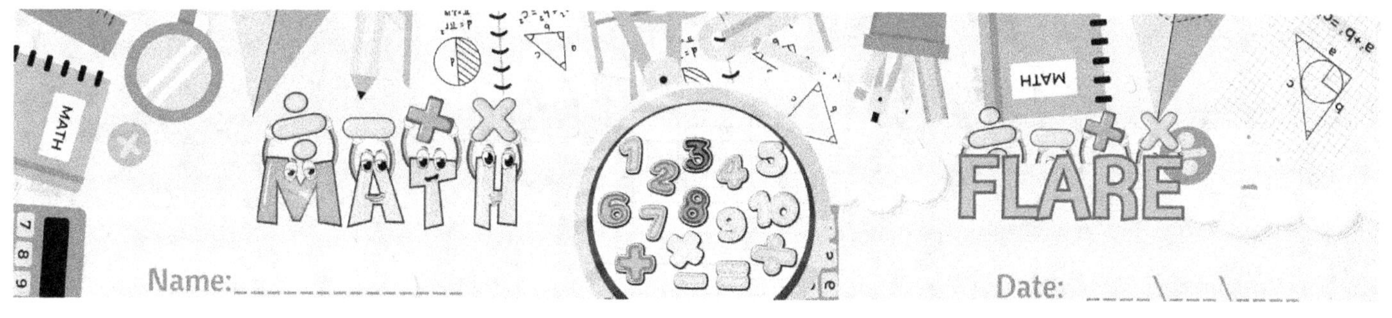

431. _____________ three thousand four hundred seventy-four

432. _____________ one thousand three hundred sixty

433. _____________ one thousand nine hundred eight

434. _____________ five thousand nine hundred fifty-one

435. _____________ four thousand nine hundred ninety

436. _____________ four thousand nine hundred seventy

437. _____________ two

438. _____________ five thousand three hundred twenty-eight

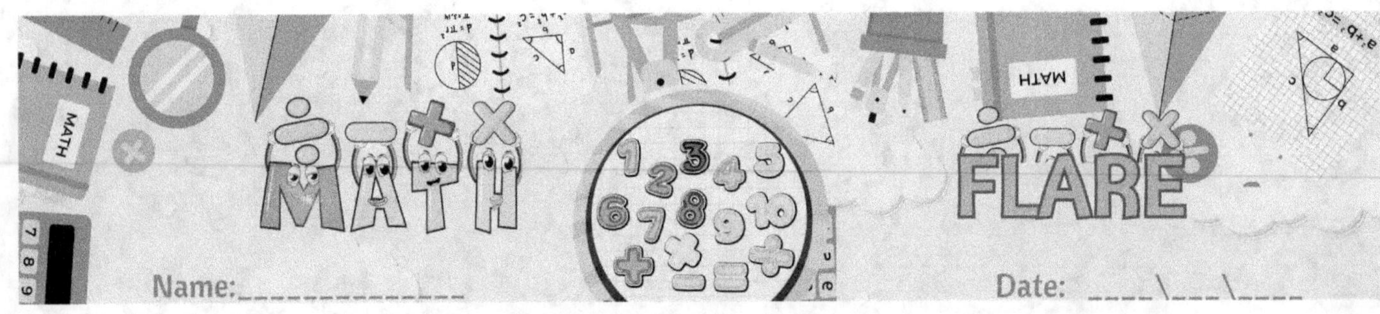

Name:_______________   Date: ____________

439. _______________ three thousand two hundred fifty-nine

440. _______________ seven thousand four hundred

441. _______________ nine thousand four hundred sixty-six

442. _______________ eight thousand thirty-four

443. _______________ six thousand eight hundred forty-four

444. _______________ two thousand four hundred forty-six

445. _______________ two thousand six hundred eighty

446. _______________ eight thousand seven hundred forty-eight

447. _______________ six thousand eight hundred eighty-seven

448. _______________ five thousand three

449. _______________ seven thousand two hundred sixteen

450. _______________ three thousand five hundred twenty-nine

451. _______________ two thousand nine hundred ninety-seven

452. _______________ nine thousand four hundred one

453. _______________ nine thousand three hundred forty-four

Place Value: Expanded Notation

Provide the expanded notation for each value.

454. 76 _______________________

455. 665 _______________________

456. 725 _______________________

457. 592 _______________________

458. 547 _______________________

459. 882 _______________________

460. 553 _______________________

461. 584 _______________________

462. 111 _______________________

463. 6 _______________________

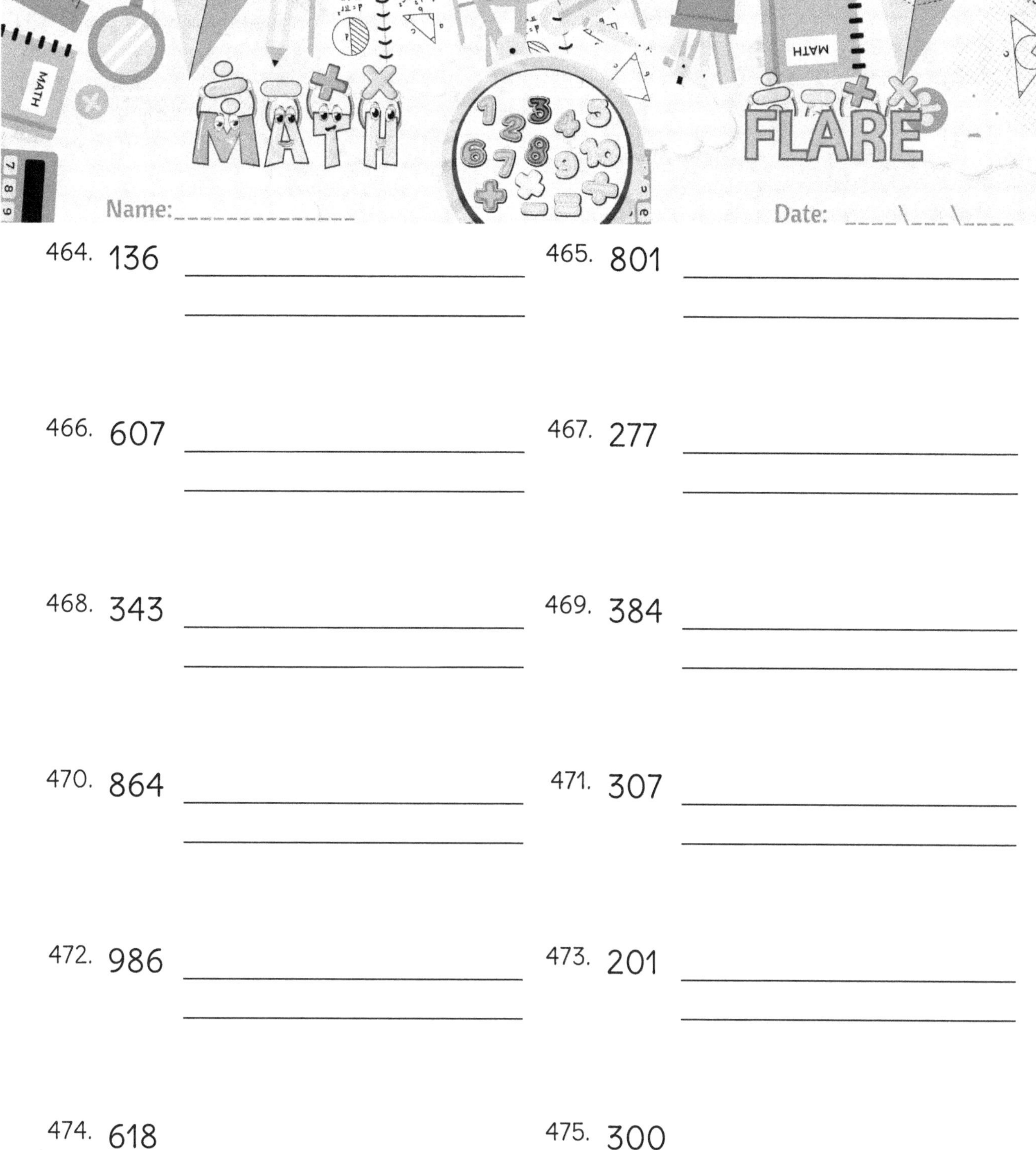

464. 136 _______________________

465. 801 _______________________

466. 607 _______________________

467. 277 _______________________

468. 343 _______________________

469. 384 _______________________

470. 864 _______________________

471. 307 _______________________

472. 986 _______________________

473. 201 _______________________

474. 618 _______________________

475. 300 _______________________

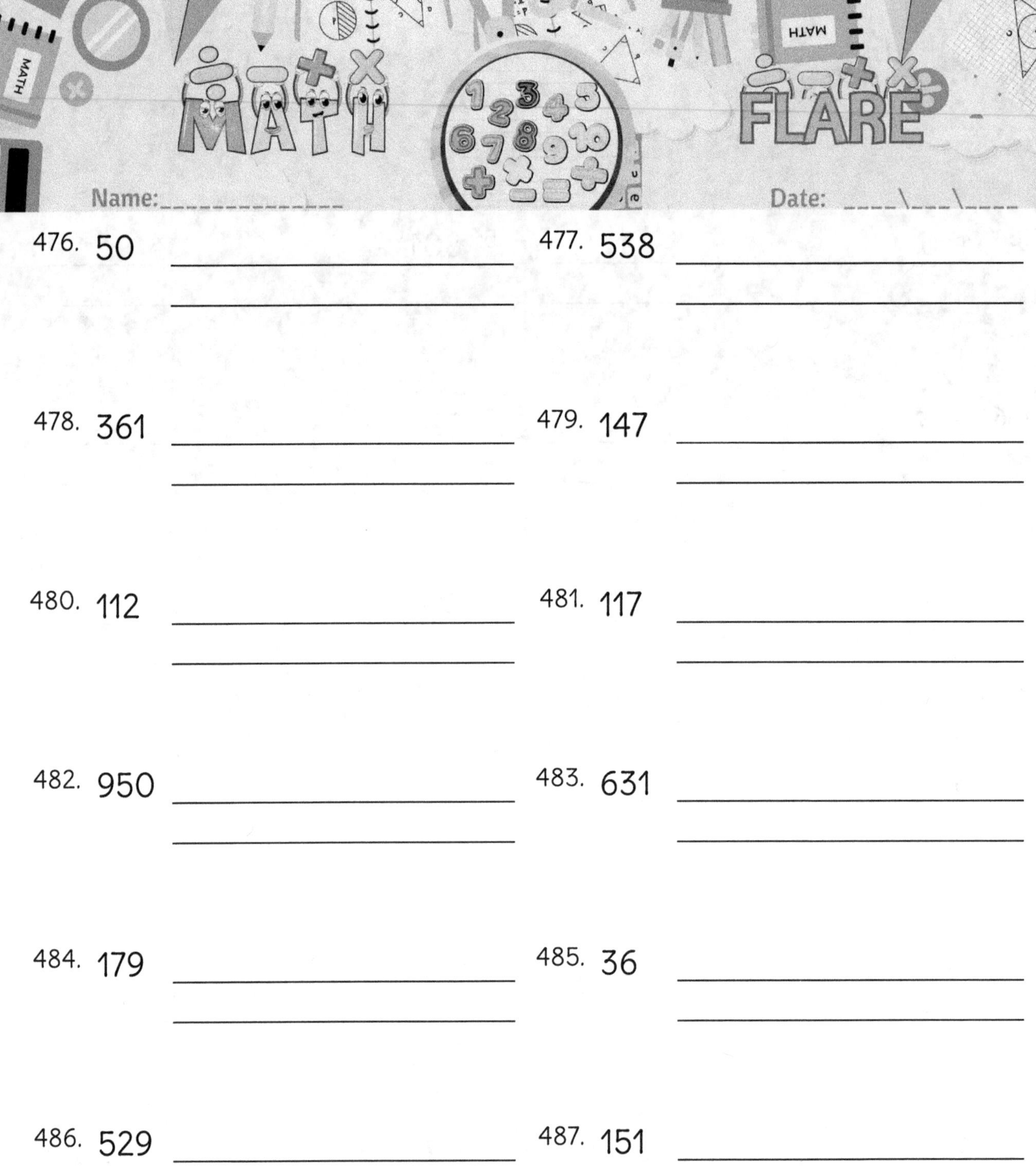

476. 50

477. 538

478. 361

479. 147

480. 112

481. 117

482. 950

483. 631

484. 179

485. 36

486. 529

487. 151

488. 325 _______________________

489. 685 _______________________

490. 840 _______________________

491. 803 _______________________

492. 460 _______________________

493. 877 _______________________

494. 475 _______________________

495. 161 _______________________

496. 503 _______________________

497. 421 _______________________

498. 581 _______________________

499. 866 _______________________

500. 326 _______________________

501. 391 _______________________

502. 848 _______________________

503. 614 _______________________

504. 123 _______________________

505. 870 _______________________

506. 244 _______________________

507. 941 _______________________

508. 362 _______________________

509. 775 _______________________

510. 616 _______________________

511. 188 _______________________

512. 233 ______________________

513. 401 ______________________

514. 771 ______________________

515. 437 ______________________

516. 633 ______________________

517. 479 ______________________

518. 826 ______________________

519. 101 ______________________

520. 273 ______________________

521. 456 ______________________

522. 951 ______________________

523. 657 ______________________

524. 543 _______________________

____

525. 62 _______________________

____

526. 846 _______________________

____

527. 110 _______________________

____

528. 458 _______________________

____

529. 797 _______________________

____

530. 628 _______________________

____

531. 956 _______________________

____

532. 493 _______________________

____

533. 819 _______________________

____

534. 720 _______________________

____

535. 268 _______________________

____

536. 337 _______________

537. 509 _______________

538. 308 _______________

539. 791 _______________

540. 587 _______________

541. 788 _______________

542. 549 _______________

543. 70 _______________

544. 653 _______________

545. 571 _______________

546. 60 _______________

547. 107 _______________

ANSWERS

Page 1: Place Value

1. 5 ones	2. 9 tens	3. 7 tens	4. 6 ones
5. 5 hundreds	6. 8 hundreds	7. 7 hundreds	8. 9 thousands
9. 2 tens	10. 1 hundred	11. 1 thousand	12. 6 tens
13. 1 hundred	14. 3 tens	15. 1 ten	16. 1 hundred
17. 4 ones	18. 1 one	19. 7 thousands	20. 4 thousands
21. 1 thousand	22. 9 hundreds	23. 6 thousands	24. 5 hundreds
25. 5 tens	26. 5 ones	27. 2 hundreds	28. 3 tens
29. 3 hundreds	30. 1 hundred	31. 3 thousands	32. 2 tens
33. 1 hundred	34. 6 tens	35. 3 thousands	36. 0 ones
37. 7 ones	38. 3 hundreds	39. 5 ones	40. 6 tens
41. 4 tens	42. 7 hundreds	43. 6 hundreds	44. 2 thousands
45. 3 tens	46. 3 hundreds	47. 8 hundreds	48. 4 tens
49. 8 hundreds	50. 1 thousand	51. 2 hundreds	52. 5 ones
53. 6 thousands	54. 9 ones	55. 3 thousands	56. 4 tens
57. 6 hundreds	58. 5 thousands	59. 1 thousand	60. 1 ten
61. 1 one	62. 9 thousands	63. 6 tens	64. 7 thousands
65. 2 hundreds	66. 2 hundreds	67. 8 tens	68. 5 ones
69. 2 hundreds	70. 8 thousands	71. 3 tens	72. 8 hundreds
73. 7 ones	74. 6 ones	75. 0 hundreds	76. 2 hundreds

77. 3 hundreds   78. 5 hundreds

Page 6: Place Value: Expanded Notation

79. 8,589	80. 6,774	81. 4,028	82. 3,650	83. 7,411
84. 5,153	85. 7,453	86. 1,551	87. 6,929	88. 1,659
89. 771	90. 9,782	91. 9,034	92. 281	93. 3,104
94. 658	95. 6,357	96. 6,539	97. 1,541	98. 4,328
99. 7,376	100. 2,621	101. 4,944	102. 7,681	103. 498
104. 7,944	105. 9,743	106. 2,449	107. 8,627	108. 175
109. 5,063	110. 8,094	111. 4,370	112. 1,437	113. 462
114. 5,243	115. 2,913	116. 6,470	117. 4,596	118. 7,918
119. 3,952	120. 7,482	121. 9,191	122. 3,428	123. 887
124. 7,730	125. 8,687	126. 2,330	127. 3,440	128. 3,875
129. 2,459	130. 5,767	131. 1,296	132. 5,670	133. 7,405
134. 5,969	135. 1,831	136. 6,346	137. 3,153	138. 9,466
139. 5,409	140. 5,004	141. 2,923	142. 6,755	143. 6,595
144. 2,677	145. 5,413	146. 7,599	147. 9,818	148. 7,860
149. 7,744	150. 9,886	151. 1,944	152. 3,622	153. 377
154. 9,894	155. 3,429	156. 1,516	157. 6,795	

Page 16: Place Value: Expanded Notation

158. 8 thousands + 9 tens

159. 2 thousands + 1 hundred + 4 ones

160. 7 thousands + 4 hundreds + 3 tens + 8 ones

161. 6 hundreds + 7 tens + 4 ones

162. 2 thousands + 5 hundreds + 4 tens + 8 ones

163. 1 hundred + 7 tens + 8 ones

164. 3 thousands + 9 hundreds + 1 ten + 1 one

165. 2 thousands + 5 hundreds + 1 ten + 9 ones

166. 2 thousands + 8 hundreds + 8 tens + 1 one

167. 6 thousands + 7 hundreds + 7 tens + 6 ones

168. 3 thousands + 3 hundreds + 5 tens + 3 ones

169. 2 thousands + 6 hundreds + 4 ones

170. 4 thousands + 1 hundred + 5 tens + 3 ones

171. 1 thousand + 1 hundred + 1 ten + 7 ones

172. 6 thousands + 4 hundreds + 4 tens + 5 ones

173. 6 thousands + 9 hundreds + 8 tens

174. 1 thousand + 3 hundreds + 4 tens + 2 ones

175. 7 thousands + 9 hundreds + 1 one

176. 1 thousand + 4 hundreds + 8 tens + 6 ones

177. 6 thousands + 4 tens + 8 ones

178. 1 hundred + 2 tens

179. 9 hundreds + 6 tens + 7 ones

180. 4 thousands + 7 hundreds + 5 tens

181. 4 thousands + 3 hundreds + 4 tens + 9 ones

182. 1 thousand + 3 hundreds + 9 tens + 5 ones

183. 8 thousands + 5 hundreds + 3 tens

184. 7 thousands + 7 hundreds + 6 tens + 9 ones

185. 8 hundreds + 3 tens + 4 ones

186. 5 thousands + 8 hundreds + 9 tens + 5 ones

187. 2 thousands + 6 hundreds + 8 tens + 1 one

188. 1 thousand + 7 hundreds + 2 tens + 2 ones

189. 6 thousands + 9 tens + 3 ones

190. 4 thousands + 7 hundreds + 8 tens + 6 ones

191. 7 thousands + 2 hundreds + 9 tens + 6 ones

192. 1 thousand + 1 hundred + 2 tens + 6 ones

193. 5 thousands + 8 hundreds + 6 tens + 6 ones

194. 3 thousands + 4 tens + 6 ones

195. 4 thousands + 3 tens + 8 ones

196. 2 thousands + 5 hundreds + 4 tens + 5 ones

197. 1 thousand + 2 hundreds + 1 ten + 6 ones

198. 1 thousand + 4 hundreds + 6 tens + 3 ones

199. 7 thousands + 7 hundreds + 4 tens + 8 ones

200. 2 thousands + 9 hundreds + 9 tens + 6 ones

201. 7 thousands + 9 hundreds + 7 tens + 7 ones

202. 8 ones

203. 1 thousand + 5 hundreds + 8 tens + 4 ones

204. 9 thousands + 6 hundreds + 1 ten + 3 ones

205. 1 thousand + 5 hundreds + 8 tens + 7 ones

206. 6 thousands + 5 hundreds + 2 tens + 8 ones

207. 6 thousands + 9 hundreds + 4 ones

208. 6 thousands + 7 hundreds + 6 tens + 9 ones

209. 2 thousands + 7 hundreds + 4 tens + 3 ones

210. 7 thousands + 5 hundreds + 3 tens + 3 ones

211. 9 thousands + 1 hundred + 2 tens + 7 ones

212. 7 thousands + 9 hundreds + 7 tens + 1 one

213. 1 thousand + 1 hundred + 3 tens + 8 ones

214. 3 thousands + 3 hundreds + 4 tens + 1 one

215. 3 thousands + 9 tens

216. 9 thousands + 2 hundreds + 7 tens + 8 ones

217. 4 thousands + 1 ten + 8 ones

218. 2 thousands + 4 hundreds + 8 ones

219. 3 thousands + 7 tens + 8 ones

220. 6 thousands + 6 hundreds + 2 tens + 3 ones

221. 2 hundreds + 2 ones

222. 5 thousands + 5 tens + 5 ones

223. 7 thousands + 2 hundreds + 5 tens + 9 ones

224. 7 thousands + 8 hundreds + 1 ten + 6 ones

225. 6 thousands + 8 hundreds + 5 tens + 6 ones

226. 9 thousands + 9 hundreds + 9 tens

227. 5 hundreds + 8 tens

228. 3 thousands + 9 hundreds + 3 tens + 5 ones

229. 7 thousands + 3 hundreds + 2 ones

230. 5 thousands + 3 hundreds + 5 tens + 7 ones

231. 2 hundreds + 7 tens + 1 one

232. 4 thousands + 5 hundreds + 8 tens + 7 ones

233. 2 thousands + 3 hundreds + 7 tens + 2 ones

234. 7 thousands + 9 hundreds + 7 tens

235. 6 thousands + 7 hundreds + 7 tens + 2 ones

Page 24: Place Value: Expanded Notation

236. 4,342	237. 9,810	238. 8,916	239. 6,183	240. 4,305
241. 8,990	242. 5,911	243. 8,978	244. 8,559	245. 5,658
246. 9,324	247. 9,987	248. 2,526	249. 9,955	250. 4,759
251. 8,526	252. 8,807	253. 8,384	254. 1,125	255. 2,795
256. 2,923	257. 2,748	258. 3,767	259. 2,758	260. 1,596
261. 5,949	262. 2,970	263. 9,466	264. 7,385	265. 7,263
266. 4,541	267. 5,600	268. 3,168	269. 6,568	270. 8,746

271. 9,467   272. 5,101   273. 6,224   274. 8,772   275. 7,633

276. 4,290   277. 6,076   278. 8,700   279. 2,159   280. 7,531

281. 4   282. 8,053   283. 3,979   284. 2,544   285. 6,830

286. 1,463   287. 6,201   288. 1,247   289. 5,175   290. 3,851

291. 1,595   292. 6,045   293. 6,159   294. 4,588   295. 8,355

Page 29:   Place Value: Expanded Notation

296. 1,000 + 300 + 20 + 2

297. 5,000 + 700 + 10 + 3

298. 9,000 + 600 + 4

299. 8,000 + 900 + 80 + 5

300. 8,000 + 8

301. 8,000 + 600 + 40

302. 9,000 + 900 + 50 + 6

303. 4,000 + 500 + 80 + 3

304. 8,000 + 300 + 20 + 3

305. 3,000 + 400 + 40 + 4

306. 1,000 + 900 + 10

307. 8,000 + 200 + 60 + 3

308. 4,000 + 400 + 30 + 6

309. 4,000 + 300 + 50 + 4

310. 8,000 + 800 + 50 + 5

311. 8,000 + 700 + 10 + 2

312. 5,000 + 300 + 80 + 3

313. 8,000 + 900 + 10 + 9

314. 7,000 + 900 + 30 + 2

315. 7,000 + 300 + 90 + 4

316. 5,000 + 800 + 70 + 7

317. 6,000 + 10 + 1

318. 4,000 + 600 + 30 + 9

319. 900 + 6

320. 3,000 + 800 + 70

321. 9,000 + 500 + 10 + 3

322. 4,000 + 500 + 80 + 5

323. 4,000 + 600 + 60

324. 800 + 9

325. 9,000 + 800 + 50

326. 3,000 + 800 + 80 + 8

327. 8,000 + 500 + 70 + 2

328. 1,000 + 20 + 9

329. 2,000 + 700 + 70 + 3

330. 7,000 + 500 + 7

331. 7,000 + 500 + 20 + 6

332. 4,000 + 400 + 50 + 2

333. 2,000 + 800 + 80 + 4

334. 6,000 + 400 + 70 + 5

335. 2,000 + 300 + 6

336. 9,000 + 200 + 30 + 7

337. 7,000 + 200 + 90 + 6

338. 2,000 + 300 + 30 + 6

339. 8,000 + 900 + 20

340. 4,000 + 700 + 30 + 3

341. 2,000 + 300 + 4

342. 6,000 + 900 + 80 + 3

343. 4,000 + 50 + 7

344. 6,000 + 900 + 40 + 4

345. 7,000 + 500 + 8

346. 4,000 + 200 + 80 + 9

347. 8,000 + 200 + 30

348. 8,000 + 900 + 80 + 9

349. 4,000 + 300 + 50 + 5

350. 700 + 20 + 2

351. 5,000 + 300 + 10 + 1

352. 1,000 + 70 + 5

353. 8,000 + 700

354. 5,000 + 100 + 10 + 5

355. 8,000 + 400 + 90 + 3

356. 4,000 + 50 + 6

357. 5,000 + 200 + 90 + 7

358. 3,000 + 700 + 70 + 4

359. 8,000 + 400 + 70 + 3

360. 9,000 + 500 + 50 + 5

361. 3,000 + 300 + 30 + 7

362. 7,000 + 200 + 30 + 5

363. 1,000 + 600 + 60 + 4

364. 6,000 + 800 + 40 + 6

365. 1,000 + 300 + 20 + 9

366. 4,000 + 200 + 60 + 1

367. 2,000 + 400 + 90 + 9

368. 2,000 + 400 + 40 + 5

369. 5,000 + 600 + 20 + 6

370. 8,000 + 100 + 50 + 6

371. 8,000 + 500 + 80

372. 3,000 + 600 + 70 + 6

373. 5,000 + 700 + 10 + 8

374. 6,000 + 100 + 70 + 2

375. 1,000 + 500 + 60 + 7

Page 36: Place Value: Expanded Notation

376. 5,633	377. 1,308	378. 2,430	379. 6,196	380. 9,732
381. 4,603	382. 8,365	383. 4,476	384. 7,044	385. 7,210
386. 2,952	387. 8,553	388. 3,651	389. 5,280	390. 1,570
391. 6,436	392. 2,565	393. 1,837	394. 9,768	395. 3,859
396. 9,862	397. 7,036	398. 7,833	399. 1,072	400. 4,289
401. 3,782	402. 9,612	403. 3,396	404. 1,717	405. 3,952
406. 5,551	407. 9,085	408. 5,616	409. 8,435	410. 9,123
411. 3,757	412. 3,816	413. 4,949	414. 4,766	415. 6,642
416. 6,333	417. 4,040	418. 8,432	419. 1,727	420. 7,085
421. 4,912	422. 4,474	423. 9,091	424. 9,722	425. 5,092
426. 7,132	427. 874	428. 6,420	429. 8,621	430. 8,595
431. 3,474	432. 1,360	433. 1,908	434. 5,951	435. 4,990
436. 4,970	437. 2	438. 5,328	439. 3,259	440. 7,400
441. 9,466	442. 8,034	443. 6,844	444. 2,446	445. 2,680
446. 8,748	447. 6,887	448. 5,003	449. 7,216	450. 3,529
451. 2,997	452. 9,401	453. 9,344		

Page 46:   Place Value: Expanded Notation

454. seventy-six

455. six hundred sixty-five

456. seven hundred twenty-five

457. five hundred ninety-two

458. five hundred forty-seven

459. eight hundred eighty-two

460. five hundred fifty-three

461. five hundred eighty-four

462. one hundred eleven

463. six

464. one hundred thirty-six

465. eight hundred one

466. six hundred seven

467. two hundred seventy-seven

468. three hundred forty-three

469. three hundred eighty-four

470. eight hundred sixty-four

471. three hundred seven

472. nine hundred eighty-six

473. two hundred one

474. six hundred eighteen

475. three hundred

476. fifty

477. five hundred thirty-eight

478. three hundred sixty-one

479. one hundred forty-seven

480. one hundred twelve

481. one hundred seventeen

482. nine hundred fifty

483. six hundred thirty-one

484. one hundred seventy-nine

485. thirty-six

486. five hundred twenty-nine

487. one hundred fifty-one

488. three hundred twenty-five

489. six hundred eighty-five

490. eight hundred forty

491. eight hundred three

492. four hundred sixty

493. eight hundred seventy-seven

494. four hundred seventy-five

495. one hundred sixty-one

496. five hundred three

497. four hundred twenty-one

498. five hundred eighty-one

499. eight hundred sixty-six

500. three hundred twenty-six

501. three hundred ninety-one

502. eight hundred forty-eight

503. six hundred fourteen

504. one hundred twenty-three

505. eight hundred seventy

506. two hundred forty-four

507. nine hundred forty-one

508. three hundred sixty-two

509. seven hundred seventy-five

510. six hundred sixteen

511. one hundred eighty-eight

512. two hundred thirty-three

513. four hundred one

514. seven hundred seventy-one

515. four hundred thirty-seven

516. six hundred thirty-three

517. four hundred seventy-nine

518. eight hundred twenty-six

519. one hundred one

520. two hundred seventy-three

521. four hundred fifty-six

522. nine hundred fifty-one

523. six hundred fifty-seven

524. five hundred forty-three

525. sixty-two

526. eight hundred forty-six

527. one hundred ten

528. four hundred fifty-eight

529. seven hundred ninety-seven

530. six hundred twenty-eight

531. nine hundred fifty-six

532. four hundred ninety-three

533. eight hundred nineteen

534. seven hundred twenty

535. two hundred sixty-eight

536. three hundred thirty-seven

537. five hundred nine

538. three hundred eight

539. seven hundred ninety-one

540. five hundred eighty-seven

541. seven hundred eighty-eight

542. five hundred forty-nine

543. seventy

544. six hundred fifty-three

545. five hundred seventy-one

546. sixty

547. one hundred seven